Who Needs Rooster?

Rob Arego

Illustrated by Reggie Holladay

Rigby®

A Harcourt Achieve Imprint

www.Rigby.com
1-800-531-5015

Rooster was not happy.
The other animals fussed
about his crowing.

"Let them wake up by themselves,"
Rooster said.
Then he got on a big blue bus
and went away.

The first morning, the animals
were very happy.
There was no Rooster to get them up.

Some animals stayed in bed until noon.
Others read all morning long.

The next day, everyone was still happy.
Who needed Rooster?

Then things started to go wrong.
Cow missed getting milked, and Hen
ran out of room in her nest.

Horse didn't eat until late,
and Pig missed feeding time.

The animals came up with a plan
to take turns waking each other up.

The first day, Cow got up
with the sun.
"Moo! Moo!" she said.
But none of the other animals got up.

"I know I can do it," said Hen
the next day.
"Cluck! Cluck!" she said.
But the other animals kept sleeping.

"This isn't a bad job," said Horse
the next day.
"Neigh! Neigh!" he said.
But no one got up.

"I can do this work," Pig said
the next day.
"Oink! Oink!" she said.
But once again, the other animals
kept sleeping.

At last the animals called Rooster on
the phone and begged him
to come back.

Rooster gets up with the sun
every morning.

All the other animals do, too!